Endorsements for the Flourish Bible Study Series

"The brilliant and beautiful mix of sound teaching, helpful charts, lists, sidebars, and appealing graphics—as well as insightful questions that get the reader into the text of Scripture—make these studies that women will want to invest time in and will look back on as time well spent."

Nancy Guthrie, Bible teacher; author, *Even Better than Eden*

"My daughter and I love using Flourish Bible Studies for our morning devotions. Lydia Brownback's faithful probing of biblical texts; insightful questions; invitations to engage in personal applications using additional biblical texts and historical contexts; and commitment to upholding the whole counsel of God as it bears on living life as a godly woman have drawn us closer to the Lord and to his word. Brownback never sidesteps hard questions or hard providences, but neither does she appeal to discourses of victimhood or therapy, which are painfully common in the genre of women's Bible studies. I cannot recommend this series highly enough. My daughter and I look forward to working through this whole series together!"

Rosaria Butterfield, Former Professor of English, Syracuse University; author, *The Gospel Comes with a House Key*

"As a women's ministry leader, I am excited about the development of the Flourish Bible Study series, which will not only prayerfully equip women to increase in biblical literacy but also come alongside them to build a systematic and comprehensive framework to become lifelong students of the word of God. This series provides visually engaging studies with accessible content that will not only strengthen the believer but the church as well."

Karen Hodge, Coordinator of Women's Ministries, Presbyterian Church in America; coauthor, *Transformed*

"Lydia Brownback is an experienced Bible teacher who has dedicated her life to ministry roles that help women (and men) grow in Christ. With a wealth of biblical, historical, and theological content, her Flourish Bible Studies are ideal for groups and individuals that are serious about the in-depth study of the word of God."

Phil and Lisa Ryken, President, Wheaton College; and his wife, Lisa

"If you're looking for rich, accessible, and deeply biblical Bible studies, this series is for you! Lydia Brownback leads her readers through different books of the Bible, providing background information, maps, timelines, and questions that probe the text in order to glean understanding and application. She settles us deeply in the context of a book as she highlights God's unfolding plan of redemption and rescue. You will learn, you will delight in God's word, and you will love our good King Jesus even more."

Courtney Doctor, Coordinator of Women's Initiatives, The Gospel Coalition; author, *From Garden to Glory* and *Steadfast*

"Lydia Brownback's Bible study series provides a faithful guide to book after book. You'll find rich insights into context and good questions to help you study and interpret the Bible. Page by page, the studies point you to respond to each passage and to love our great and gracious God. I will recommend the Flourish series for years to come for those looking for a wise, Christ-centered study that leads toward the goal of being transformed by the word."

Taylor Turkington, Bible teacher; Director, BibleEquipping.org

"Lydia Brownback has a contagious love for the Bible. Not only is she fluent in the best of biblical scholarship in the last generation, but her writing is accessible to the simplest of readers. She has the rare ability of being clear without being reductionistic. I anticipate many women indeed will flourish through her trustworthy guidance in this series."

David Mathis, Senior Teacher and Executive Editor, desiringGod.org; Pastor, Cities Church, Saint Paul, Minnesota; author, *Habits of Grace*

COLOSSIANS

Flourish Bible Study Series
By Lydia Brownback

Judges: The Path from Chaos to Kingship

Esther: The Hidden Hand of God

Job: Trusting God When Suffering Comes

Jonah: God's Relentless Grace

Habakkuk: Learning to Live by Faith

Luke: Good News of Great Joy

Ephesians: Growing in Christ

Philippians: Living for Christ

Colossians: Fullness of Life in Christ

James: Walking in Wisdom

1–2 Peter: Living Hope in a Hard World

**FLOURISH
BIBLE STUDY**

COLOSSIANS

FULLNESS OF LIFE IN CHRIST

LYDIA BROWNBACK

WHEATON, ILLINOIS

Colossians: Fullness of Life in Christ

© 2024 by Lydia Brownback

Published by Crossway
            1300 Crescent Street
            Wheaton, Illinois 60187

Cover design: Crystal Courtney

First printing 2024

Printed in China

All emphases in Scripture quotations have been added by the author.

Trade paperback ISBN: 978-1-4335-8327-8

Crossway is a publishing ministry of Good News Publishers.

RRDS   33 32 31 30 29 28 27 26 25 24
15 14 13 12 11 10 9 8 7 6 5 4 3 2 1

With gratitude to God
for
Lauren Whalen,
the daughter I've always wanted
but never thought I'd have.

"He is before all things, and in him
all things hold together." —Colossians 1:17

CONTENTS

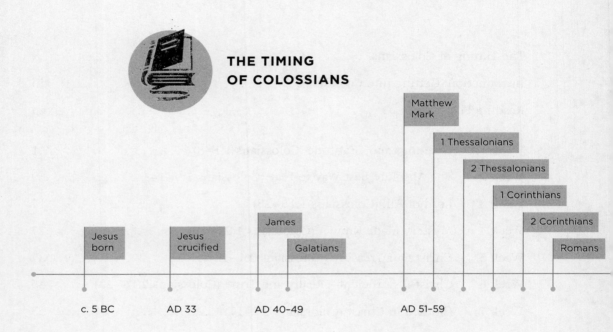

THE TIMING OF COLOSSIANS

Matthew
Mark

1 Thessalonians

2 Thessalonians

1 Corinthians

2 Corinthians

Romans

James

Galatians

Jesus born

Jesus crucified

c. 5 BC

AD 33

AD 40–49

AD 51–59

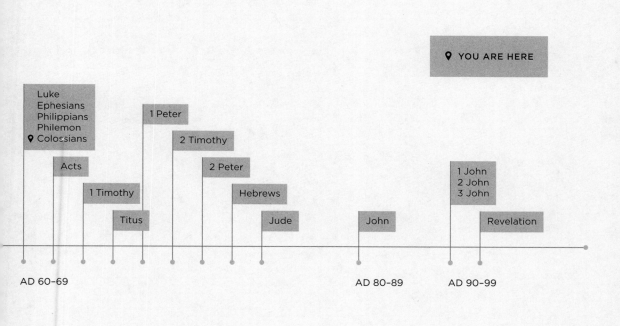

YOU ARE HERE

Luke
Ephesians
Philippians
Philemon
Colossians

1 Peter

2 Timothy

Acts

1 Timothy

2 Peter

Titus

Hebrews

Jude

John

1 John
2 John
3 John

Revelation

AD 60–69

AD 80–89

AD 90–99

INTRODUCTION

GETTING INTO COLOSSIANS

Jesus Christ is everything—there's no better way to describe the heart of this New Testament epistle, Colossians. Its message is a breath of fresh spiritual air in our sin-saturated, self-oriented age that seeks to diminish Christ or do away with him altogether. Today, even within some of our churches, Christ is sidelined, held up as nothing more than an example of a good guy on whom we can model our lives and loves. Colossians keeps us from being tricked into believing that Christ isn't sufficient for salvation. It guards us against messages claiming that what's needed is Christ plus our own best efforts, or Christ plus modern science, or Christ plus politics. The apostle Paul wrote this letter because lies about the gospel were poisoning the church at Colossae, and he was passionate to remind the believers there that the one true gospel was all they needed for, well, everything. The reminder he gave them is also for us, and how very much we need it! Whenever we hear that Jesus isn't enough for us—and we hear it all the time now—encouragement is there for us in this letter written to help our ancient brothers and sisters in Colossae. God's word to them is also his word to us.

WHO'S WHO IN COLOSSIANS

The overarching figure in Colossians is, of course, the Lord Jesus Christ. He is exalted here, held up in all his excellence and glory, perhaps more than in any New Testament letter. Also prominent is the apostle Paul, who, as the author of the letter, leads us into deeper understanding of Christ and what it means to live the Christian life. We also find mention of Paul's ministry partners, including Timothy, Epaphras, and Onesimus. We must also include here the recipients of the letter—believers in Colossae and its neighboring city Laodicea.

SETTING

Paul probably wrote the letter in AD 62 from Rome, where he was in prison because of his faith. Most likely he'd never met the believers in

Colossae. The church there had been planted some years earlier while Paul was doing ministry in Ephesus. Historians believe that during those years, a man named Epaphras traveled from Colossae, his hometown, and became a believer through Paul's teaching. Afterward, Epaphras went home to Colossae, where he shared his newfound faith and planted the Colossian church. Epaphras stayed integrally connected to Paul, and it was through this connection that Paul found out how the Colossian church was being corrupted, stirring him to address the situation and encourage the Colossian believers to hold fast to the true gospel. Most likely Paul dictated the letter to Timothy, and then his ministry partners Tychicus and Onesimus carried the letter to Colossae on Paul's behalf.

THEMES

The overarching theme of Colossians is that Christ is Lord of everything and everyone. God sent his Son, Jesus Christ, to reconcile all who put their faith in him, and those redeemed by Christ are taken spiritually into his death and resurrection, and then live their lives in and through him. The letter also shows us how the gospel was revealed over time, how it unfolded and eventually came to light in all its fullness. Now that salvation through Christ is fully known, believers can live out these spiritual realities in their day-to-day lives, growing up in their faith and sharing the wonders of salvation with a watching world.

Pronunciation Guide

Colossae	coll-AH-see	**Laodicea**	LAY-oh-diss-EE-ah
Epaphras	eh-PAPH-russ	**Hierapolis**	hire-OP-olis
asceticism	ah-SET-ah-cism	**Demas**	DEE-muss
Scythian	SITH-ee-an	**Archippus**	are-KIPP-iss
Tychicus	TICK-a-kiss	**Onesimus**	oh-NESS-a-miss
Aristarchus	heiress-TARK-iss		

The Setting of Colossians (c. AD 62)[1]

STUDYING COLOSSIANS

At the beginning of each week's lesson, read the entire passage. And then read it again. If you are studying Colossians with a group, read it once more, aloud, when you gather to discuss the lesson. Marinating in the Scripture text is the most important part of any Bible study.

GROUP STUDY

If you are doing this study as part of a group, you'll want to finish each week's lesson before the group meeting. You can work your way through the study questions all in one sitting or by doing a little bit each day. And don't be discouraged if you don't have sufficient time to answer every question. Just do as much as you can, knowing that the more you do, the more you'll learn. No matter how much of the study you are able to complete each week, the group will benefit simply from your presence, so don't skip the gathering if you can't finish! That being said, group time will be most rewarding for every participant if you have done the lesson in advance.

If you are leading the group, you can download the free leader's guide at https://www.lydiabrownback.com/flourish-series.

Marinating in the Scripture text is the most important part of any Bible study.

INDIVIDUAL STUDY

The study is designed to run for ten weeks, but you can set your own pace if you're studying solo. And you can download the free leader's guide (https://www.lydiabrownback.com/flourish-series) if you'd like some guidance along the way.

	Reading Plan	
	Primary Text	**Supplemental Reading**
Week 1	Colossians 1:1–8	Acts 9:3–19
Week 2	Colossians 1:9–14	
Week 3	Colossians 1:15–23	Proverbs 8:22–31
Week 4	Colossians 1:24–29	Genesis 12:1–3; Galatians 3:7–9
Week 5	Colossians 2:1–15	Proverbs 2:3–5; Romans 2:25–29
Week 6	Colossians 2:16–23	
Week 7	Colossians 3:1–17	
Week 8	Colossians 3:18–4:1	Philemon 1–25
Week 9	Colossians 4:2–6	
Week 10	Colossians 4:7–18	Revelation 3:14–19

GREETINGS AND GRATITUDE

COLOSSIANS 1:1-8

Wouldn't you agree that there's always a bit of anticipation in going to the mailbox to get the daily delivery? You never know when you might discover a personalized letter or a greeting card hiding among all the junk mail and bills. Sometimes, though, the greetings aren't really all that personal but just pretend to be—like those holiday cards from your lawn-care service or local politician. Since the senders don't really know us, the greetings they convey ring hollow. The apostle Paul didn't know many of the believers at Colossae, but his letter is deeply personal even so. From the very start, we pick up on his genuinely warm tone. It's clear he's writing to those he considers true friends. How revealing this is about the bond of true faith! In union with Christ, believers are not only friends but also family—the sort of bond that's typically unhindered by time and geographical distance. Paul's heart is filled with gratitude and genuine love for the Colossian Christians, and this week we find out why.

1. GRACE-FILLED GREETINGS (1:1-2)

Paul begins Colossians as he does most of his letters, identifying both the senders and the recipients, and expressing his desire that those to whom he is writing will experience God's grace and peace, the blessings of his unearned favor:

> "Paul, an apostle of Christ Jesus by the will of God, and Timothy our brother, To the saints and faithful brothers in Christ at Colossae: Grace to you and peace from God our Father." (vv. 1–2)

✦ Before getting into the substance of the letter, Paul gives his credentials. He was an apostle, one of the spiritual leaders of the early Christian church. Read Acts 9:3–19, the story of Paul's conversion (he was known as Saul at the time). What in this story explains why Paul attributes his call as an apostle to God's will?

....

....

....

....

....

....

....

Apostles
The apostles were men specifically chosen by Christ and given authority to establish and lead the early church. Each apostle had seen the risen Christ firsthand. There are no apostles today.

✦ What do you think Paul was communicating to the recipients of the letter by sharing his credentials?

....

....

....

....

....

Paul includes Timothy in his greeting. It's possible that Timothy served as Paul's secretary for this letter, writing down the words Paul dictated to him. We don't know for sure the role Timothy played in writing the letter, but we do know that he was a vital partner in Paul's ministry. He traveled with Paul on missions trips (Acts 16:1–20:4), and on at least one occasion he served as Paul's spokesman (1 Corinthians 4:15–17). He also preached alongside Paul (2 Corinthians 1:19).

✦ What do we learn from Paul's greeting about how he views the believers at Colossae?

When Paul describes the Colossian believers as "saints," he's not saying that they had achieved a super-high level of spiritual maturity. In reality, all who belong to Christ by faith, no matter their level of growth, are saints. They are "set apart" ones, chosen by God for salvation.

2. GRATITUDE FOR GOD'S GRACE (1:3-6)

Paul begins, as he so often does in his letters, with gratitude. His words of thanksgiving aren't a mere formality, but a reminder that God is the source—the very reason—for the Colossians' salvation and all the blessings that come along with it:

> We always thank God, the Father of our Lord Jesus Christ, when we pray for you, since we heard of your faith in Christ Jesus and of the love that you have for all the saints, because of the hope laid up for you in heaven. Of this you have heard before in the word of the truth, the gospel, which has come to you, as indeed in the whole world it is bearing fruit and increasing—as it also does among you, since the day you heard it and understood the grace of God in truth. (vv. 3–6)

✦ As Christians, we also thank God for our many blessings. Do you offer regular thanks for the things Paul expresses here? For what do you most frequently give thanks to God?

✦ What two qualities does Paul attribute to the Colossian believers in verse 4?

    1. ....

    2. ....

Paul roots these two qualities in hope, specifically the hope laid up for believers in heaven (v. 5). The sort of hope Paul has in mind here isn't primarily an emotion or a sense of well-being. The hope he is writing about is an actual reality, all the blessings of salvation that begin in this lifetime but won't be fully known and experienced until we are home in heaven for eternity.

✦ Colossians is not the only letter in which the apostle Paul links faith, love, and hope. What does each of the following passages add to our understanding about how faith, love, and hope work together?

    · 1 Corinthians 13:1–13

    · Galatians 5:5–6

    · Ephesians 4:1–6

· 1 Thessalonians 5:8

The hope laid up in heaven is a vital aspect of "the word of the truth" (v. 5), which is the gospel. The word *gospel* means "good news," and in the Bible, the good news—the gospel—is that sinners are saved through the death and resurrection of Jesus Christ. And this good news is not a secret, revealed to only a select few. At the time Colossians was written, the gospel had already spread to places like Syria, Greece, Italy, North Africa, and beyond, which is what Paul means by "the whole world" in verse 6.

Paul says that the gospel is "bearing fruit" (v. 6). The metaphor of fruit bearing goes all the way back to the beginning, to the time of creation, when God told Adam and Eve to "be fruitful and multiply" (Genesis 1:28). What began then as *biological* fruit bearing—generations of children and grandchildren growing over time into a great nation—eventually expanded into *spiritual* fruit bearing, growing God's family by means of salvation in Jesus.

✦ The fruit bearing Paul has in mind in verse 6 isn't just about outsiders coming into God's family; it's also about an ongoing process in believers' lives. How do Jesus's words in John 15:1–5 show us how this fruit bearing happens?

Salvation is by grace alone—*that* is the gospel truth, contrary to what false teachers were trying to spread around the church at Colossae. Paul reassures the Colossians that they have understood the gospel correctly, calling it "the grace of God in truth" (v. 6). God's grace is his determination to save and bless undeserving sinners. No one deserves God's favor; in fact, each one of us deserves the opposite—God's wrath. So without grace, there would be no gospel, no good news.

✦ In another one of his letters, Paul goes into a bit more detail about the grace that undergirds the gospel. How does Ephesians 2:1–9 deepen your understanding of gospel grace?

3. GRATITUDE FOR GOSPEL GROWTH (1:7–8)

We discover in verse 7 that the Colossians learned the gospel from Paul's friend and ministry associate Epaphras, a shortened form of the name Epaphroditus. Epaphras was himself a Colossian.

> ". . . just as you learned it from Epaphras our beloved fellow servant. He is a faithful minister of Christ on your behalf and has made known to us your love in the Spirit." (vv. 7–8)

✦ What do we learn about Epaphras's relationship with the Colossian believers in verses 7 and 8?

✦ Twice in the first eight verses of this letter Paul notes the Colossians' love. In verse 4, he comments on the love they have for other believers, and here in verse 8, he references their "love in the Spirit." How do 2 Corinthians 13:14 and Philippians 2:1 shed light on what Paul means by "love in the Spirit"?

LET'S TALK

1. Paul was characterized by gratitude. He expresses thanks for the faith, love, and hope of fellow believers, for the spread of the gospel, and for his partners in ministry. Expressing gratitude to God for all our blessings is, of course, good and right, but Paul shows us that genuine godly gratitude extends beyond our personal blessings. Discuss what makes you thankful. Do your reasons for gratitude align with Paul's?

2. Review how Paul weaves faith, love, and hope together in Colossians 1:3–6. How has hope impacted your faith and your ability to love others? Include in your discussion the other end of the spectrum, hopelessness. If you've experienced a season of hopelessness, what impact has that had on your faith and relationships? What does Paul say in this passage that can restore lost hope?

THE ABSOLUTE BEST WAY TO PRAY

COLOSSIANS 1:9–14

"I'll pray about that!" It's a good thing to say when a friend shares about a challenge she is facing or, for that matter, any time someone tells us about an unmet need or crisis. But do we actually pray? "I'll pray for you" can all too easily become little more than a polite response rather than a promise to be kept. I've tried to make it a practice never to say, "I'll pray for you," unless I actually intend to carve out time to do it. But even then, I fall far short of the apostle Paul, whose passion for Christ's people compelled his prayers. "From the day we heard, we have not ceased to pray for you," he writes to the Colossians in this week's passage. Some of what fueled his prayers for them was concern about what was happening in the Colossian church. As we noted in the introduction, newcomers were promoting wrong teaching about God and the gospel, causing confusion. Knowing this behind-the-scenes situation helps us make sense of why Paul prays as he does in the prayer we'll study together this week.

1. PRAYER FOR A WORTHY WALK (1:9–10)

Even though Paul had never met the Christians at Colossae, he prayed for them on a regular basis. He might not have known them personally, but their shared union with Christ ignited in Paul a love and affection for the Colossians that went as deep as the closest family bond. That's why, at the beginning of his letter to them, Paul writes, "We always thank God . . . when we pray for you" (v. 3). Now, in verses 9–10, he gets more specific about how he prays for them:

"And so, from the day we heard, we have not ceased to pray for you, asking that you may be filled with the knowledge of his will in all spiritual wisdom and understanding, so as to walk in a manner worthy of the Lord, fully pleasing to him: bearing fruit in every good work and increasing in the knowledge of God." (vv. 9–10)

The false teachers in Colossae were claiming to have some sort of special knowledge about God and the path to salvation, which is why Paul prays that his Colossian friends will be filled with true, Spirit-given knowledge. The specific knowledge he prays for is an understanding of God's will. Of course, we all want to know God's will for our lives, but what we're often looking for are details about where we should live or whom we should marry. That's quite different from what Paul has in mind here. The will of God that Paul prays we would know isn't divine revelation about the specifics of our lives but rather how to shape our entire lives—plans, priorities, choices—around God's purposes and priorities.

Fill in the "The Will of God" chart that follows, noting what each passage reveals about God's will, and then write a summary statement of what it means to discover God's will for the various choices and decisions of our lives.

The Will of God	
Deuteronomy 29:29	
Psalm 40:8	
Romans 8:26–27	
Ephesians 1:5–9	
1 Thessalonians 4:3	
1 Thessalonians 5:18	
Hebrews 10:5–10	

1 Peter 2:15	
1 Peter 3:14–17	

✤ Summary: The way to know God's will in the choices and decisions I face is:

....

....

....

....

Looking at all these passages enables us to understand why true knowledge of God's will is shaped by "spiritual wisdom and understanding" (v. 9). When we live with people, we become attuned to their likes and dislikes, their preferences and pleasures. In the same way, growing in our knowledge of God tunes us to his character and his overarching purposes, not only for our individual lives but also for all creation for all time. In the process, we develop a taste for how to make God-guided decisions in personal matters big and small.

✤ According to verse 10, what three fruits will develop in our lives as we grow in the knowledge of God's will?

1. ....

2. ....

3. ....

✤ When you seek to know God's will, are these fruits your primary goal? If not, what *are* you seeking?

....

....

2. PRAYER FOR SPIRITUAL STRENGTH (1:11–12)

Paul prays not only that his Colossian brothers and sisters will grow deep in the knowledge of God but also that this knowledge will bring about more spiritual growth:

> ". . . being strengthened with all power, according to his glorious might, for all endurance and patience with joy; giving thanks to the Father, who has qualified you to share in the inheritance of the saints in light." (vv. 11–12)

✣ According to verse 11, what is the "power" Paul has in mind?

✣ We don't typically link joy with patience and endurance. If we're honest, we'll settle for the ability to just smile and press on with daily life when we have to endure some difficulty. Read in Acts 5:12–42 about what happened to the apostles when they had to endure unjust treatment. What does this story in Acts show you about the power Paul writes of here in Colossians 1:11?

✣ According to verse 12, why is thankfulness a fitting response to everything we experience, including difficulties and hardships?

....

....

Paul's prayer is so convicting! Most of us regularly thank God for prospering our lives, and we even trustingly thank him for his care when things don't go so well. But no matter what condition we find ourselves in, do we offer thanks for our spiritual inheritance? It's hard to do when we are caught up in the here and now, which is the very reason Paul prays that they will be caught up in the things of Christ. The spiritual growth that Paul prays for is supernatural, a work of God's Spirit enabling gratitude that extends beyond our temporal concerns to our eternal blessings.

3. DELIVERED! (1:13–14)

Paul's reference to an inheritance in verse 12 likely comes from his knowledge of the Old Testament, where the word *inheritance* refers to the promised land. This prosperous land, Canaan, was set apart by God as a place for his very own people to live and grow and worship as they dwelt securely in the blessings of his covenant with them. Paul views that Old Testament inheritance as a pattern, a foreshadowing, of what God's people inherit through their union with Christ in the new-covenant era.

> "He has delivered us from the domain of darkness and transferred us to the kingdom of his beloved Son, in whom we have redemption, the forgiveness of sins." (vv. 13–14)

✙ What does Ephesians 4:17–19 reveal about life in this "domain of darkness?"

....

....

....

....

✙ How does Colossians 1:14 explain what Paul means by "delivered" and "transferred" in verse 13?

....

....

LET'S TALK

1. Do you pray for those you've promised to pray for? Of course, we can't possibly pray for every concern that crosses our paths. Talk about how to make realistic prayer commitments. Consider also how often your prayers for people, and for yourself, consist of the sorts of things Paul prays for. Ask the Lord to reshape your heart so that your desires in prayer reflect Paul's.

2. What principles do you apply when you are faced with the need to make a choice between various good options? Discuss what you learned this week about how to choose biblically.

LORD OF ALL!

COLOSSIANS 1:15-23

When I was a little girl, I loved to watch my mother prepare for a glamorous night out. She'd sit at her dressing table and apply makeup—eye shadow, lipstick—and then spritz on a bit of Chanel Nº 5. At the very end, she'd open her jewelry case and make a selection. I remember one such occasion vividly. Just as she opened the case, the sun, which was lowering on the western horizon, sent a beam through the window that alighted on a tangle of gems. The entire room was suddenly ablaze, dots and shimmers of light dancing on the walls and ceiling. I was mesmerized. No doubt, in the moment, my mother explained how rays of light travel through gemstones, refracting as they do, but I was too caught up in the spectacle cast by those jewels to care about the science behind it. Even more beautiful is the splendor of the Lord Jesus Christ, which Paul puts on full display this week. He describes the Lord with majestic, highly exalted words. Some Bible scholars think Paul's description of Christ in this passage was adapted from an early Christian hymn. Whatever his inspiration might have been, Paul took great care with his words in order to magnify Christ in all his fullness and glory. Our goal isn't to admire Paul's artistry but, by meditating on his beautiful words, to grow the same passion for Christ so visible here.

1. LORD OF CREATION (1:15-17)

Paul's beautiful description has two basic parts. In the first half, verses 15–17, Christ is exalted as Lord of creation:

"He is the image of the invisible God, the firstborn of all creation. For by him all things were created, in heaven and on earth, visible and invisible, whether thrones or dominions or rulers or authorities—all things were created through him and for him. And he is before all things, and in him all things hold together." (vv. 15–17)

✦ As we begin, isolate the two "He is . . ." declarations about Christ from this first half of the "hymn."

· He is . . .

· He is . . .

The facets of Christ that Paul holds out in his description can best be understood from other Bible passages. Continuing with our jewelry metaphor, think of how the multi-faceted cut of a diamond reveals its depth and color and beauty more than if the jewel were merely flat. In a similar way, other scriptures reveal facets of the gloriousness of Christ in Paul's description.

✦ What "facet" does Hebrews 1:1–4 add to Paul's words here in Colossians 1:15–17?

✦ It seems likely that when Paul wrote this section of Colossians, he had in mind a poem from Proverbs that describes how God created the world through wisdom. Although it's probably best not to view that Proverbs poem as a direct reference to Christ, the description there is reflected in what Paul writes about Christ here in Colossians. What do you learn about creation from Proverbs 8:22–31, and how is that seen here in Colossians 1:15–17?

Metaphor

"A figure of speech in which a word or phrase literally denoting one kind of object or idea is used in place of another to suggest a likeness or analogy between them."[2]

In verse 15, Paul describes Jesus Christ as "the *firstborn* of all creation" (v. 15), and as we'll see in the second half of the poem, he describes him as "the *firstborn* from the dead" (v. 18). We want to clarify that by describing Christ as "firstborn," Paul isn't saying that the Son of God came into being the way everyone else does. Although he was born as a man (what theologians call "the incarnation"), Christ, the Son of God, has always existed. So when Paul uses the term "firstborn," he's referring to the rights and privileges that, in Bible times, were granted to a first male child.

✦ What do we learn about Christ's role in creation and the purpose for creation from verse 16?

· Christ's role:

· Purpose for creation:

....

....

✤ Look back at the two "he is . . ." declarations that you isolated at the beginning of this section. What does Paul's use of the present-tense verb "is" reveal about Christ's person and work?

....

....

....

....

2. LORD OF THE CHURCH (1:18–20)

In the second part of Paul's "hymn," Christ's authority over God's people, the church, is on display. The church Paul is speaking of here is made up of all genuine believers, those who have been united to Christ by faith:

> "And he is the head of the body, the church. He is the beginning, the firstborn from the dead, that in everything he might be preeminent. For in him all the fullness of God was pleased to dwell, and through him to reconcile to himself all things, whether on earth or in heaven, making peace by the blood of his cross." (vv. 18–20)

✤ Isolate the "He is . . ." declarations about Christ in this second half of Paul's "hymn."

· He is . . .

....

· He is . . .

....

✤ The first "He is" declaration introduces another metaphor—God's people, the church, as a body, and Christ as the head of that body. As you think about how a human body functions, what does Paul's metaphor convey about both Christ and Christians?

✦ Read 1 Corinthians 12:12–27, another place where Paul makes use of his "body" metaphor. What does this passage add to our understanding about the relationship of Christ and believers, and what this relationship means for how we live out our faith?

✦ Paul begins the next "He is" declaration noting that Christ himself is "the beginning"—not God's first creation but the one who began creation.[3] And then once again Paul names Christ as "firstborn." Just as we saw in the last section, "firstborn" here isn't about physical birth but about rights and status. Paul makes this clear when he writes that Christ is "the firstborn from the dead, *that in everything he might be preeminent*" (v. 18). A preeminent person is at the very top; there is no one higher. How does 1 Corinthians 15:20–26 shed light on Christ's status as firstborn from the dead?

✦ God's overarching plans and purposes for creation, from the beginning of time until the final judgment, center on Christ. That's the emphasis of Paul's "hymn," and we see it clearly in verse 19, where he says that in Christ, "all the fullness of God was pleased to dwell." Paul mentions this "fullness" again a bit later in the letter, in Colossians 2:9. As you consider 1:19 and 2:9 together, how would you summarize this "fullness of God" in your own words?

✦ What purpose of God's does Paul declare in verse 20, and how was this purpose achieved?

3. LORD OF SALVATION (1:21–23)

Christ is the center of everything and the God-appointed means through which God accomplishes all his purposes. That's what Paul has so beautifully expressed in his description. Now Paul brings these magnificent truths to bear on our own lives and guides us how to respond:

> "And you, who once were alienated and hostile in mind, doing evil deeds, he has now reconciled in his body of flesh by his death, in order to present you holy and blameless and above reproach before him, if indeed you continue in the faith, stable and steadfast, not shifting from the hope of the gospel that you heard, which has been proclaimed in all creation under heaven, and of which I, Paul, became a minister." (vv. 21–23)

✦ "Alienated and hostile"—that was us before we were saved. We might not have felt hostile toward God, but the truth lies not in what feels or seems true but in what the Bible tells us. According to Paul here, in what particular way was our former hostility manifested?

....

....

....

....

✤ How does Ephesians 2:1–3 help us understand the nature of this alienation and hostility?

....

....

....

....

✤ According to verse 22, what was God's purpose for reconciling us through Christ's death?

....

....

....

....

We find an "if clause" in verse 23: we will be found holy and blameless "*if* indeed you continue in the faith." Paul certainly isn't saying we have to work for our salvation. That would undo everything he has just proclaimed, which is that Christ alone saves us. Paul's point is that by our continuing in the faith, we prove that we've been reconciled.

....

"The only proof of past conversion
is present convertedness."[4]

....

✤ What two words does Paul use in verse 23 to express what it means to "continue in the faith."

✤ Look again at the whole of verse 23 and then summarize in your own words what it means to "continue in the faith."

The better we know Christ, the more we will love him and build our lives around him. We know this is true from Paul's own example here in the letter. His grasp of the gospel worked into his heart the love and awe expressed in his beautiful "hymn" of praise.

LET'S TALK

1. This portion of Colossians is heavy on doctrine and can seem to be a bit of a "theological ivory tower" when we first approach it. But there are actually a ton of practical takeaways from Paul's exalted teaching about Christ here. As you think about *how* Paul expresses these truths—his passion, his carefully chosen words, his exalted tone—what does this show you about his heart for God? Discuss the link between Paul's knowledge of God and the gospel and his passion for Christ, and then identify some practical ways to more firmly establish that link for yourself.

2. Our natural tendency is to view most people as "pretty good." Discuss how a fuller view of Christ changes our thinking not only about Christ himself but also about human beings in general. Consider how we approach people with the gospel. Do we feel more urgency to share the good news with those who seem to be the worst sinners, or do we recognize that polished unbelievers who have their worldly act together are equally hostile and in need of salvation?

MYSTERY MADE KNOWN

COLOSSIANS 1:24-29

Springtime is a mood lifter, wouldn't you agree? When light overtakes the evening hours and warm sunshine caresses the days, in the blink of an eye, bare branches are green and buds are in bloom. And then one morning we look outside and everything's lush and bursting white, pink, and yellow. Full spring is right before our eyes, even though the moment-by-moment unfolding of it was elusive. The mystery of springtime. That's a bit like how the gospel came in all its fullness. Paul describes it as a mystery once hidden but now revealed, and this week we'll see what he means. Not only have the riches of Christ been revealed—they have come to us! The delights of the gospel are far superior to the delights of springtime, and we rejoice in our salvation. Even so, joy seems to evaporate when disappointments and daily frustrations mount up. But it doesn't have to be that way, as Paul shows us. He viewed everything in his life—good things and bad—through the lens of the gospel, so he was characterized by contentment and joy. He saw even his suffering as an opportunity to magnify Christ.

1. STEWARDING THE MYSTERY (1:24-26)

Paul opens up about the suffering he experiences in his ministry:

> "Now I rejoice in my sufferings for your sake, and in my flesh I am filling up what is lacking in Christ's afflictions for the sake of his body, that is, the church, of which I became a minister according to the stewardship from God that was given to me for you, to make the word of God fully known, the mystery hidden for ages and generations but now revealed to his saints." (vv. 24–26)

✦ Paul actually rejoices when he suffers. Do a quick read through the first twenty-three verses of the letter. Based on what and how he has written so far, what do you think enables Paul to have this outlook on his suffering?

....

....

....

....

✦ How does verse 24 reveal Paul's love for fellow Christians?

....

....

....

....

You might be perplexed by what Paul means when he writes, "I am filling up what is lacking in Christ's afflictions." Does he mean that somehow all that Christ suffered to atone for our sin wasn't quite enough? In other words, is there something that Paul is adding to Christ's redeeming work, or that we have to add, in order to complete what Christ started? Well, we know that can't be true because of all Paul has just written! The

> **Bible Study Principle**
>
> Less clear texts can be understood by considering texts that are clearer.

theme of his letter up to this point has been the absolute sufficiency of Christ for our salvation. So what does he mean? To help us understand, we can apply a general principle of Bible study: *less clear texts can be understood by considering texts that are clearer.* As we apply that principle—in this case, through examining other New Testament Epistles—it becomes evident that Paul is talking about the suffering that Christians experience because they are Christ's people, his body (v. 24).

🍃 How do the following passages shed light on the afflictions Paul has in mind in verse 24?

· Philippians 3:7–10

....

....

....

....

· 1 Peter 4:12–14

....

....

....

....

🍃 Read Acts 9:10–19, which you first read back in Week 1. What happened at the time of Paul's conversion (when he went by the name of Saul) to give him his current mindset about his suffering?

....

....

....

....

🍃 We recall that Paul is writing this letter while he is imprisoned—one of the ways in which he suffered for his faith. What is revealed in 2 Corinthians 11:24–28 about other kinds of suffering he experienced?

....

....

✦ Paul views his ministry as a "stewardship from God." A steward in the Roman world of Paul's day was the administrator or manager of a large household or estate.[5] Paul's use of this term reveals a lot about his place not only in the lives of the Colossian believers but in the early church in general. What was the primary responsibility of this stewardship he was given?

Paul refers to the word of God, the gospel, as a "mystery." This is the first of four times Paul uses the word *mystery* in the letter. He's not using the word the way we think of it, as a puzzle or riddle to solve by seeking out hidden clues. Paul uses "mystery" to indicate that God revealed to people over time what he had planned from eternity past—the gospel, the salvation of sinners through Jesus Christ. Most likely he chose to use this particular word as a contrast to the false teachers who were saying that salvation could come only through their own brand of secret, mysterious knowledge. The first time Paul uses the word, here in verse 26, he says that the mystery of the gospel was hidden in times past but has now been revealed to Christians (saints) in the present. Of course, the gospel wasn't completely hidden from God's people until Christ came—there are glimpses of it all through the Old Testament—but it was veiled, not yet fully revealed.

2. MYSTERY REVEALED (1:27)
Paul shows more facets of this gospel "mystery" the second time he uses the word:

> "To them God chose to make known how great among the Gentiles are the riches of the glory of this mystery, which is Christ in you, the hope of glory." (v. 27)

The unfolding of the mystery reveals that Gentiles—those outside of Israel—have been brought into full gospel riches. In our time, when God's people aren't distinguished by birth lineage, it's hard to get why this was such a big deal. Knowing some key Old Testament background helps us understand. Beginning with Abraham, God set apart certain people to live in a covenant relationship with him. These people became the nation of Israel. Under the gracious oversight of God, his people Israel were to keep his covenant by living holy lives, which included separation from people, the Gentiles, who didn't worship the one true God.

✦ With this background in mind, how does Genesis 12:1–3, together with Galatians 3:7–9, show the slow unveiling of how Gentiles were grafted in among God's people?

✦ How does Colossians 1:27 summarize the essence of this gospel mystery?

> ### The Hope of Glory
>
> "We are all so identified with Christ that it is impossible for any Christian to be a second-class citizen. And we can add to this grace the fact that our hope of glory in Jesus has present and future aspects. In the present, we are assured that we belong to him and will persevere so that in the future we will enjoy the full benefits of redemption—life in a resurrected body before the presence of God in the new heaven and earth."[6]

✦ How does Ephesians 1:1–10 explain what Paul means by "Christ in you" in Colossians 1:27?

....

....

....

....

3. STRONG IN CHRIST'S STRENGTH (1:28-29)

Paul wants his Colossian friends to understand the purpose of his suffering, that the Lord actually uses the hardships Paul experiences in ministry to spread far and wide the mystery now revealed—the atoning and redeeming work of Christ that's completely sufficient to save sinners from among every tribe and nation and ethnicity. So now he tells them the intended outcome, the goal of his labors, and why it's totally worth it:

> "Him we proclaim, warning everyone and teaching everyone with all wisdom, that we may present everyone mature in Christ. For this I toil, struggling with all his energy that he powerfully works within me." (vv. 28–29)

✦ Based on what we've learned this week so far, summarize what Paul means when he says that Christ himself is what he proclaims.

....

....

....

....

✦ What does Paul say in verse 28 about *what* he does, *how* he does it, and *who* receives his ministry labors?

....

....

....

....

✟ Paul uses the word *wisdom* six times in this letter (1:9; 1:28; 2:3; 2:23; 3:16; and 4:5). Think about the situation that motivated Paul to write to the believers at Colossae (to refresh your memory, take a quick look back at the "Setting" and "Themes" sections in the introduction). How do the happenings in the Colossian church shed light on why he uses this word *wisdom* so frequently in the letter?

> "[Paul] was reliant upon God. He was dependent upon God. He rested in God's strength. He strove by grace. He did the work God gave him. What causes us to burn out in our professions? Relying on our own strength and working on things which God has not gifted us to do. When we do what he would have us do, and when we are reliant upon his grace, we mount up on wings as eagles, and we can do great works, hard works, strivings for God, dependent on his grace and strength."[7]

✟ What overarching reason does Paul give for why he proclaims Christ?

✦ In light of all the suffering Paul experiences in ministry, how does verse 29 show why he is able to press on with so much zeal?

....

....

....

....

LET'S TALK

1. Read 1 Peter 4:1–2, where the apostle Peter, like Paul, links Christ's suffering to the suffering of Christians. Peter writes that "whoever has suffered in the flesh has ceased from sin" (v. 1), but he certainly doesn't mean that our suffering serves as an antidote to sin. His point is that "when believers are willing to suffer, the nerve center of sin is severed in their lives."[8] Discuss how seasons of suffering in your life have worked to mature you spiritually.

....

....

....

....

....

....

....

....

2. Paul attributes his perseverance in ministry to divine power, which is worked into him (Colossians 1:29), yet such power wasn't reserved just for the apostles. Read Ephesians 1:15–19 and Philippians 4:11–13. How do these passages shed light on how this divine power is available to us as well? Discuss ways in which increased awareness of the enabling you

have in Christ can help you overcome discouragement in your Christian walk and renew your zeal to proclaim Christ in what you say and how you live.

CHRIST OUR TREASURE

COLOSSIANS 2:1-15

Among my favorite childhood memories are the treasure hunts my mother wove regularly into her gift giving, from Valentine's candy to birthday presents. Each treasure hunt began with a clue that she'd written on a folded-up piece of paper. This clue sent us to the next clue and, from there, to another and another until the gift was finally revealed. Some of these hunts took a long time (at least, it seemed that way in our child minds), but we persevered, even through the more challenging clues, because, while we didn't know what awaited us at the end, we *did* know it was going to be something really good. These simple treasures of childhood were a small taste of the infinitely valuable spiritual treasure we believers seek:

> "Yes, if you call out for insight
>> and raise your voice for understanding,
> if you seek it like silver
>> and search for it as for hidden treasures,
> then you will understand the fear of the Lord
>> and find the knowledge of God." (Proverbs 2:3–5)

What we find at the end of this search is Jesus Christ himself. There's no need to look beyond him, to hunt for more, because there is no greater treasure. To continue our metaphor, the Colossian believers had found Christ, but they were being lured toward a new batch of clues that would lead them away from, not toward, the treasure they'd already found. This danger was what prompted Paul's letter, and, as we'll see this week, he is passionate to keep them centered on the treasure of Christ.

1. REACHING THE RICHES (2:1–5)

Paul intends the message of his letter to reach not just the believers at Colossae but also those in the nearby city of Laodicea and likely others who were closely affiliated with the Colossian church. It's clear from his words that he genuinely loves these Christians, even those he has never met in person:

> "For I want you to know how great a struggle I have for you and for those at Laodicea and for all who have not seen me face to face, that their hearts may be encouraged, being knit together in love, to reach all the riches of full assurance of understanding and the knowledge of God's mystery, which is Christ, in whom are hidden all the treasures of wisdom and knowledge. I say this in order that no one may delude you with plausible arguments. For though I am absent in body, yet I am with you in spirit, rejoicing to see your good order and the firmness of your faith in Christ." (vv. 1–5)

🕊 At the end of last week's lesson, when we came to the end of Colossians 1, Paul was describing his ministry efforts. He continues that description here at the beginning of Colossians 2 (it's actually quite seamless, as there were no chapter or verse divisions in his original letter). In 1:29 and 2:1, he describes his efforts as "toil" and "struggle," even though he's empowered by divine strength. How does the situation in the Colossian church, as well as Paul's heart for these believers, explain why he sees his labor on their behalf as a struggle?

....

....

....

....

🕊 Paul describes the goal of his toil in verse 2. What four aspects of his goal can you identify from verse 2?

1. ....

2. ....

3. ....

4. ....

✦ What accompanies the kind of love Paul names in verse 2?

✦ Paul links believers' assurance—confidence of salvation in Christ and of being kept securely by him for eternity—to their understanding of the gospel. What about the gospel message provides such assurance?

We find the word *mystery* again in verse 2, which Paul here applies directly to Christ himself. Then, in verse 3, he identifies two things that are "hidden" in Christ. This is a good reminder of how Paul uses the word *mystery*—to describe something once hidden but now revealed. In this case, the "treasures" hidden in Christ are wisdom and knowledge.

✦ How does 1 Corinthians 1:24–30 shed more light on the treasure of wisdom that's ours in Christ?

Paul's mention of "knowledge" in verse 3 gets to the heart of his concern. The false teachers in Colossae claimed that they possessed a secret, hidden knowledge that was necessary for salvation, and Paul wants to make very clear that the only saving knowledge necessary for salvation is found in Christ and his gospel.

✦ According to verse 4, how might the false teachers ensnare people, and what in verse 5 is shown to be the antidote to this snare?

2. ROOTED IN CHRIST (2:6–10)

When our beliefs and convictions are tested and challenged, we need some guiding principles to strengthen our faith and help us continue walking in God's ways. The Colossians were facing such challenges, so in this next section, Paul instructs them how to stand firm:

> "Therefore, as you received Christ Jesus the Lord, so walk in him, rooted and built up in him and established in the faith, just as you were taught, abounding in thanksgiving. See to it that no one takes you captive by philosophy and empty deceit, according to human tradition, according to the elemental spirits of the world, and not according to Christ. For in him the whole fullness of deity dwells bodily, and you have been filled in him, who is the head of all rule and authority." (vv. 6–10)

Christians are those who have received Christ; they have been united to him by faith. And because that's true—"therefore" (v. 6)—they have all they need to press ahead.

✦ In verses 6 and 7, Paul gives instructions for how to live a Christ-centered life. What images does he use, and what are they intended to convey?

✦ Paul issues a warning in verse 8, urging the Colossians to guard against being captivated by false teaching. What do you think it means to become captivated in this way?

....

....

....

....

We are given a huge clue in verse 8 about the nature of the false teaching threatening the Colossian church. It was undergirded with powerful intellectual arguments— "philosophy"—and what Paul labels "empty deceit," which is teaching that is worthless and untrue. The "human tradition" and "elemental spirits" Paul names have to do with ungodly worldliness that produces nothing but corruption. Whatever the specifics of the false teaching, its basic premise watered down the gospel and painted Christ alone as insufficient for salvation.

✦ Paul makes his case using two forms of the word *fill* in verses 9 and 10. How does his use of this word counter the basic premise of the false teaching that Christ is insufficient for salvation?

....

....

....

....

When Christ came to live on earth, he took on flesh. He didn't lose his deity in the process. Instead, he added to it a human nature. He became the God-man, both fully divine and fully human. And when he ascended back to heaven after his resurrection, he didn't lose his human nature, his flesh. He will be both God and man for all eternity. That's why Paul writes that "in him the whole fullness of deity dwells bodily" (v. 9).

3. A NEW POSITION (2:11–15)

Paul continues to unfold the spiritual blessings we have in Christ and how being united to him changes everything about us. A primary change is our *position*:

"In him also you were circumcised with a circumcision made without hands, by putting off the body of the flesh, by the circumcision of Christ, having been buried with him in baptism, in which you were also raised with him through faith in the powerful working of God, who raised him from the dead. And you, who were dead in your trespasses and the uncircumcision of your flesh, God made alive together with him, having forgiven us all our trespasses, by canceling the record of debt that stood against us with its legal demands. This he set aside, nailing it to the cross. He disarmed the rulers and authorities and put them to open shame, by triumphing over them in him." (vv. 11–15)

First, we see that our position has changed from uncircumcised to circumcised. (Of course, Paul is just using the Old Testament rite of circumcision as a metaphor!) To make sense of why he chooses this imagery, read Genesis 17:9–14, where God establishes his covenant with Abraham. From that point on, circumcision became the distinctive mark that set apart Israel, the Jews, as God's own special people.

✦ Now, with that bit of history in mind, read Romans 2:25–29, another passage where Paul uses circumcision imagery to make a point about salvation in Christ. What do the backstory in Genesis and Paul's words in Romans add to your understanding of what Paul means here in Colossians 2:11?

In verse 12, Paul helps us understand why Christians undertake the rite of baptism. Water baptism symbolizes our identity with Christ in his death. It points to the fact that our position is now *in* Christ. In the same way, Christ's resurrection from the dead has changed our position from being dead in our sin to being alive in him.

Incarnation

"The incarnation wasn't something that happened two thousand years ago, and then ended approximately thirty-three years later. He didn't lose his physicality or any other part of His human nature when he ascended to be with His Father in heaven, as if it were something to be despised. The Son of God, without giving up His deity, became a perfect man, and is still a perfect man, in glory. The One who now sits enthroned in the heavens is God, yes, but He is also the perfect human being. And we, if we are united to Him by faith, will one day become perfect in our humanity, on the day we see him face to face."[9]

In verses 13 and 14, we see glimpses of a doctrine that theologians call *substitutionary atonement*. This doctrine exposes the debt we owe to God for our sin—a debt we could never pay because the cost is our very life. So God in his kindness canceled our debt through Christ's death on the cross. Jesus took our place as our substitute and paid our debt with his own life. The term Paul uses here, "record of debt," is a word picture for each person's indebtedness to God because of sin. "God himself has mercifully resolved this problem for all who put their faith in Jesus by taking this note and nailing it to the cross, where Jesus paid the debt. The image comes from the notice fastened to a cross by the Roman authorities, declaring the crime for which the criminal was being executed."[10]

✝ Through Christ's death on the cross, God also defeated every demonic power— "rulers and authorities" (v. 15)—that seeks to hold us bound in sin and destroy our lives. Note the terms Paul uses in verse 15 to describe this spiritual victory. What implications do these terms have for how we are meant to live out our faith in our day-to-day lives?

"Dying and rising with Christ signifies death to the power of sin and Satan plus empowerment to live the new life that Jesus calls believers to live in imitation of him."[11]

LET'S TALK

1. We learned this week that Christ is the one who has "all the treasures of wisdom and knowledge" (v. 3). In things you have seen, heard, or read recently, can you identify teaching that claims to be wise and knowledgeable but is actually unwise? Talk about why such teaching can captivate people and make inroads even inside churches. Include in your discussion some practical ways to discern between truth and error.

2. Paul instructs, "As you received Christ Jesus the Lord, so walk in him, rooted and built up in him and established in the faith, just as you were taught, abounding in thanksgiving" (vv. 6–7). How are you doing this, both individually and alongside others in your church? Be specific.

CHRIST IS SUFFICIENT—
REALLY AND TRULY

COLOSSIANS 2:16-23

Try harder, be better, do more. If you've ever tried to live under the weight of that modern mantra, you know it leads only to exhaustion and discouragement. We strive to achieve, to control, but the effort just leaves us overwhelmed, frustrated, and joyless. It simply doesn't work, and that's because it's not supposed to. God designed us to live in the achievement of Christ and under his control. Yet even when we know this truth, we can fall into the control trap. Our daily exposure to empowerment messages and "You got this!" memes can compel us toward do-it-yourself discipleship and tempt us to believe that growth in Christ rests on our own efforts. The Colossians were falling into a very similar trap. False teachers were trying to persuade them that Christ wasn't sufficient to save them, so if they really wanted to be saved, they had to adopt certain practices and follow certain rules. So Paul claims in no uncertain terms that Christ is all they—and we—need. As we'll see, there is no need to pay any attention to teaching that roots our standing with God in our own efforts.

1. ONLY SHADOWS (2:16-17)

Paul's entire focus so far has been Christ—the absolute sufficiency of Christ for salvation. And because he is sufficient, nothing else—no behavior or observance—is needed from us. Now, in this section, he begins to expose the false teachers and debunk their message:

"Therefore let no one pass judgment on you in questions of food and drink, or with regard to a festival or a new moon or a Sabbath. These are a shadow of the things to come, but the substance belongs to Christ." (vv. 16–17)

✜ The Colossians must not allow anyone to "pass judgment" on them because they no longer practice the ceremonies and rituals of the Old Testament law. What does it mean to "pass judgment" on someone?

....

....

....

....

Paul names three practices from the Old Testament: festivals, new moons, and Sabbaths (most likely Israel's sabbatical holidays). These were practices stipulated in the law of Moses, in the Mosaic covenant. (If you want to dig a bit deeper, you can learn about the specific old-covenant festivals in Leviticus 23.) Paul's mention of "a new moon" is most likely a reference to Israelite festivals that began on the first of the month, a date set by the lunar cycle. All these rituals and practices were required before Christ came, but Christ's work on the cross abolished those old-covenant requirements and ushered in a new covenant, the same one we live by today.

> *Under the old covenant, being right with God required God's people to keep the law and make sacrifices when they failed. Under the new covenant, God's people have been declared right with him because Christ kept the law and sacrificed himself.*

✜ Paul says that we aren't to let others "pass judgment" on us regarding what we eat and drink. How is this brought out more fully in Romans 14:13–19?

....

....

....

....

Paul reminds his friends that all those Old Testament practices were merely a "shadow" of things to come (v. 17). If you ever took a literature class, you might remember a literary technique called "foreshadowing." When an author gives hints early in the story about what will happen at the end, she is foreshadowing. She doesn't tell us exactly what will happen, but she crafts her story in such a way that there are subtly veiled clues—shadows—of what will be fully revealed later in the story. The storyline of the Bible contains a lot of foreshadowing about the person and work of Jesus Christ. In fact, everything in the Old Testament points to Christ. That's what Paul is getting at when he says that all those laws and rituals were "a shadow of the things to come, but the substance belongs to Christ."

"Human beings are often attracted to dramatic acts of self-denial in their search for peace and for God. However, the message of the gospel refutes all such attempts to make a grand gesture for God. God has already accomplished all that is required in Christ, and so there is nothing further that can be done. Even those of us who have believed the gospel can be led to believe that externals are what matter most to God. If that begins to happen, we must be confronted with reality just as Paul confronted the Colossians. And the best way for that to happen is to do just what Paul did: present the true gospel again in its simplicity and completeness."[12]

2. QUALIFIED FOR GROWTH (2:18–19)

Paul warns most especially about one particular false teacher in this week's passage, most likely the ringleader of the bad teachers in Colossae. From Paul's words here, we get a glimpse of this troublesome person:

> "Let no one disqualify you, insisting on asceticism and worship of angels, going on in detail about visions, puffed up without reason by his sensuous mind, and not holding fast to the Head, from whom the whole body, nourished and knit together through its joints and ligaments, grows with a growth that is from God." (vv. 18–19)

✦ What does Paul reveal about the character of this particular false teacher?

✦ How does 1 Corinthians 9:24–27 shed light on how buying into false teaching can "disqualify" someone?

The false teacher and his followers were saying that true Christians are those who practice "asceticism." In other words, they were teaching that full acceptance with God requires radical self-denial, like fasting from food and adopting other restrictive behaviors. And the teaching included the idea that practicing these rigid behaviors would open a door to angels and secure angelic help and security.

✦ How does Paul debunk the false teaching in verse 19?

Asceticism

Asceticism is "the practice of strict self-denial as a measure of personal and especially spiritual discipline."[13]

✛ Look closely at Paul's metaphor of the human body in verse 19, a metaphor we first considered back in Week 3. Note again here what this metaphor conveys about our spiritual growth.

✛ Read Ephesians 4:10–16, another "body" passage. Jot down any additional insights provided in this passage about the importance of Christian fellowship.

3. A VERY GOOD QUESTION (2:20-23)

When we want answers, we ask questions. But sometimes we ask questions not because we need answers but simply as a way to get people to think. Paul asks one of these "rhetorical" questions in these next verses:

"If with Christ you died to the elemental spirits of the world, why, as if you were still alive in the world, do you submit to regulations—'Do not handle,

Do not taste, Do not touch' (referring to things that all perish as they are used)—according to human precepts and teachings? These have indeed an appearance of wisdom in promoting self-made religion and asceticism and severity to the body, but they are of no value in stopping the indulgence of the flesh." (vv. 20–23)

"*Wherever authentic, joyful confidence in Christ diminishes, regulations are brought in to preserve what the power of Christ once created.*"[14]

✝ Paul mentioned these "elemental spirits" earlier, in verse 8, and we noted that the term implies ungodly worldliness, which corrupts how people think and behave. What reminder does Paul give here in verse 20 about what changes a Christian's relationship to things in the world?

✝ Some of the Colossians were falling into the false teachers' trap—"Do not handle, Do not taste, Do not touch" (v. 21). We've learned that these prohibitions had to do with Old Testament dietary laws and worship practices. How does verse 17 show the way that we are to view these old regulations?

You've likely heard it said that "God helps those who help themselves," but this supposedly wise saying is actually unwise, because it opposes the gospel. The truly wise are those who know they can do nothing to save themselves or to earn God's favor. That's what Paul is getting at in verse 23 as he exposes the trap set by the false teachers, who were saying that radical self-denial heightens spiritual experience.

✦ How do Jesus's words in Mark 7:14–23 help us make sense of Colossians 2:23, where Paul says that "self-made religion and asceticism and severity to the body . . . are of no value in stopping the indulgence of the flesh"?

LET'S TALK

1. Paul warned the Colossians that when they live out their faith with a good conscience, they mustn't let others pass judgment on them and make them feel guilty (v. 16). Discuss some practical ways we can guard our hearts against others' judgment. In turn, is there a situation or relationship in which you've judged others? Discuss how this week's study reshapes our perspective.

2. We might not be tempted to pick up Old Testament festivals and dietary laws or to worship angels today, but other ideologies can pull us away from complete reliance on Christ. Think, for example, about political ideologies and health-care mandates. Can you think of other beliefs or behaviors that can affect our reliance on Christ alone for security?

_____

_____

_____

_____

_____

_____

_____

_____

CLOTHED IN CHRIST

COLOSSIANS 3:1-17

An angst-filled text from a friend abruptly changed my plans one rainy afternoon. My friend, during a morning walk earlier that day, had somehow lost her engagement ring. Was I free to join her as she retraced her steps? "I'd be glad to help," I told her as I averted my eyes from the rain beating hard against the window. Three hours later, we were soaked to the skin and, because her walk route had passed through a cow pasture, covered in muck. I peeled off those disgusting clothes the moment I got home. (We never did find that ring.) Clean jeans and a T-shirt felt so utterly fresh, like they were brand-new. Perhaps you've had a similar experience, and, if so, you'll appreciate how Paul describes our Christian growth in this week's lesson. He identifies the dirty, sinful practices we must put off, and then, having been washed clean by Christ, the fresh, new practices that we must put on.

1. LIVE WHERE YOU ARE (3:1–4)

Christ being seated at God's right hand is a mark of authority. His position indicates that he rules the world and everything in it. And because we are united to him by faith, we are, in a spiritual sense, right there with him even as we live out our lives here on earth. Spiritually speaking, we went with him into death and were raised into God's heavenly kingdom:

> "If then you have been raised with Christ, seek the things that are above, where Christ is, seated at the right hand of God. Set your minds on things that are

above, not on things that are on earth. For you have died, and your life is hidden with Christ in God. When Christ who is your life appears, then you also will appear with him in glory." (vv. 1–4)

✤ Being united to Christ by faith means that we have died with him and have been raised with him. Here in these verses, what does Paul say are the implications of both of these realities?

....

....

....

....

✤ The way we think significantly shapes the way we live, which is why the Bible tells us to be good stewards of our thought life. How are we called to do this in verse 2?

....

....

....

....

✤ Twice in this passage Paul references "things that are above." What do you think this phrase means?

....

....

....

....

✤ For a fuller biblical picture of how we are to govern our thought life, fill in the Mind Renewal Chart that follows by summarizing what each passage says about how we are to think.

Mind Renewal Chart	
Colossians 3:2	Let Scripture rather than the world around me shape how I view things.
Isaiah 26:3	
Romans 8:5-7	
Romans 12:2	
Philippians 3:13-15	
Philippians 4:8	

2. PURGE OUT THE OLD (3:5–11)

Our place and position with Christ are meant to shape the way we live:

> "Put to death therefore what is earthly in you: sexual immorality, impurity, passion, evil desire, and covetousness, which is idolatry. On account of these the wrath of God is coming. In these you too once walked, when you were living in them. But now you must put them all away: anger, wrath, malice, slander, and obscene talk from your mouth. Do not lie to one another, seeing that you have put off the old self with its practices and have put on the new self, which is being renewed in knowledge after the image of its creator. Here there is not Greek and Jew, circumcised and uncircumcised, barbarian, Scythian, slave, free; but Christ is all, and in all." (vv. 5–11)

We see here how to work out practically, in our lives and relationships, the spiritual transformation that has already occurred. As Paul says, because the person we used to be before Christ claimed us *has died*, we are to *put to death* the remnants of our sinful selves that remain.

Posse Non Peccare

"Prior to the fall, we were able to sin or not to sin." The early church father Augustine called this *posse peccare* or *posse non peccare* (Augustine's Latin phrasing). When Adam and Eve fell, humanity lost the ability not to sin, and ever since humans have been dead in sin and trespasses, and remain that way unless or "until the Lord sovereignly intervenes to give us new spiritual life." When we are born again, "we regain the ability not to sin (*posse non peccare*), but that does not mean we will be sinless. Until we are brought into God's presence, sin remains," so we will need to fight against it for the rest of our earthly lives.[15]

Killing off our lingering sin tendencies isn't just about identifying bad habits and working hard to crush them. Paul isn't advocating a self-improvement program. After all, there is nothing uniquely Christian about self-improvement. The truth is that before we are united to Christ, we aren't able not to sin. In union with him, we are able not to sin, even though we still do. Do you see the difference? It's the basis for Paul's instructions here.

✝ Paul gives a list of "earthly" characteristics, specific patterns of sin, in verse 5, and he tells us to put them to death. How do the following passages help us see how?

· Matthew 5:29–30

· Romans 6:12–13

· Romans 13:14

· Galatians 5:16

✝ Paul adds to his vice list in verses 8–9. What do these additional vices all have in common?

Thus far, Paul has described sin killing as "put to death" (v. 5) and "put . . . away" (v. 8). Now, in verses 9 and 10, he encourages us with a clothing metaphor meant to remind us of our spiritual status. Being *in Christ* means we have "put off" the old self and "put on" the new self, so we increasingly reflect the one we are united to (v. 10).

🕊 Verse 10 tells us that our transformation into Christlikeness occurs as we are "renewed in knowledge." Keeping in mind that one of Paul's primary purposes in writing this letter is to debunk false knowledge, what sort of knowledge do you think he has in mind here?

....

....

....

....

The Scythians, people whom Paul mentions in verse 11, resided along the northern coast of the Black Sea. The Scythians were held in contempt by more cultured people in Paul's day. Paul's point is that Christ is the great leveler. The worldly distinctions that divide people—gender, race, ethnicity, socioeconomic status—lose their divisive power among Christians.

3. LIVE WHAT YOU ARE (3:12-17)

Building on his clothing metaphor, Paul describes how to grow up into spiritual maturity:

> "Put on then, as God's chosen ones, holy and beloved, compassionate hearts, kindness, humility, meekness, and patience, bearing with one another and, if one has a complaint against another, forgiving each other; as the Lord has forgiven you, so you also must forgive. And above all these put on love, which binds everything together in perfect harmony. And let the peace of Christ rule in your hearts, to which indeed you were called in one body. And be thankful. Let the word of Christ dwell in you richly, teaching and admonishing one another in all wisdom, singing psalms and hymns and spiritual songs, with thankfulness in your hearts to God. And whatever you do, in word or deed, do everything in the name of the Lord Jesus, giving thanks to God the Father through him." (vv. 12–17)

🕊 When you consider the lifestyle Paul describes here, what do you think is his objective? In other words, who is most affected when these qualities are lived out—and when they are not?

_____

_____

_____

_____

✢ Notice how many times thankfulness is mentioned in this passage. Based on what you see here, describe the ways gratitude plays a role in our spiritual growth.

_____

_____

_____

_____

No area of life is excluded from Christ's lordship. That's what Paul means when he says that all we say and do is to be done "in the name of the Lord Jesus" (v. 17).

LET'S TALK

1. Setting our minds on "things that are above" doesn't require us to avoid everything that isn't explicitly Christian, so what does it require? Talk about the ways in which your daily intake of books, television, and social media is shaping your passions and priorities. How can you establish and maintain Christ-mindedness?

_____

_____

_____

_____

_____

2. Have you ever noticed the kinship you feel toward the people in your church, even those who are different from you? Clothes and cars, place and position—somehow those distinctions fall away in the fellowship of God's people. There's a Spirit-given recognition that we're all part of the same family. Describe the differences in your experiences of gathering with fellow believers and gathering with those who don't know Christ. What do the differences in those experiences reveal about Christ and his purposes for his people?

WHATEVER YOU DO . . .

COLOSSIANS 3:18-4:1

Fathers were the heads of households in Paul's day, providing oversight for every member, including slaves or servants, although mothers took an active role in child-raising. Typical homes were made up of mother, father, and children, and many homes included slaves or bondservants as well. In the portion of his letter we'll be studying this week, Paul addresses all these household members in pairs. In each pair—wives and husbands, children and parents, bondservants and masters—one is subordinate and the other is authoritative. Regardless of one's position, each is called to reflect Christlikeness. Similar instructions to those Paul gives here, what Bible scholars call a "household code," are found in his letter to the Ephesians (5:22–6:9). We'll see that in each pairing, Paul addresses the subordinate ones first—not as a way to demand more from them but likely as a way to show that they have equal value and worth to the authorities they must obey. To our modern ears, Paul's teaching here might seem way too authoritarian and narrow, but his approach was actually quite radical for his time, an age that offered few rights and protections to vulnerable people.

1. WIVES AND HUSBANDS (3:18-19)

Paul's blueprint for godly marriage is short and to the point:

> "Wives, submit to your husbands, as is fitting in the Lord. Husbands, love your wives, and do not be harsh with them." (3:18–19)

✛ Paul roots his instruction to wives—that they submit to their husbands—in what best reflects their faith and the Lord they worship. How do the following passages shed light on what Paul means by "fitting in the Lord"?

· Ephesians 5:22–24

....

....

....

....

· 1 Peter 3:1–2

....

....

....

....

✛ Next is a two-part instruction for how Christian husbands are to lead their marriage: they are to love their wives and avoid harshness. How do the following passages enrich your understanding of Paul's teaching here?

· Ephesians 5:25–30

....

....

....

....

· 1 Peter 3:7

....

....

....

....

✤ How can marriages that are lived out as Paul instructs here in Colossians reveal the character of God and serve as signposts to the gospel?

....

....

....

....

2. CHILDREN AND PARENTS (3:20-21)

Paul's second pairing is children and parents:

> "Children, obey your parents in everything, for this pleases the Lord. Fathers, do not provoke your children, lest they become discouraged." (3:20–21)

Children obeying parents seems logical and reasonable to most people, not just Christians. After all, parents have the benefit of age and experience to know what's best. Even so, Paul grounds his instruction to children not in this natural reason but in God himself.

✤ Paul's rationale for children's obedience goes all the way back to the Ten Commandments, the fifth of which concerns children and parents (Exodus 20:12). In another one of his letters, he repeats this instruction for children and bolsters his argument by quoting the fifth commandment more fully (Ephesians 6:2–3). How do those two passages explain his rationale here in Colossians?

....

....

....

....

....

While children are called to obey both father and mother equally, Paul directs his parental instructions exclusively to fathers since, in those days, fathers were the recognized household authority.

✦ In what ways do you think a father might "provoke" his children to the point of discouragement?

....

....

....

....

✦ What do Paul's instructions in verses 18–21 indicate about God's heart for families and individual family members?

· Husbands

....

....

....

....

· Wives

....

....

....

....

Honoring Parents

The fifth commandment "is the first and only of the Ten Commandments to contain a promise. . . . In the new covenant the promise of the land is not physical land on earth but eternal life, which begins when one is regenerated here and now and comes to full reality in the age to come. Paul is not teaching salvation on the basis of works. The obedience of children is evidence that they know God, and it results in receiving blessings from God."[16]

· Mothers

....

....

....

....

· Fathers

....

....

....

....

· Families

....

....

....

....

3. BONDSERVANTS AND MASTERS (3:22–4:1)

Paul has more to say to bondservants and masters than to any of the others in his household code:

> "Bondservants, obey in everything those who are your earthly masters, not by way of eye-service, as people-pleasers, but with sincerity of heart, fearing the Lord. Whatever you do, work heartily, as for the Lord and not for men, knowing that from the Lord you will receive the inheritance as your reward. You are serving the Lord Christ. For the wrongdoer will be paid back for the wrong he has done, and there is no partiality. Masters, treat your bondservants justly and fairly, knowing that you also have a Master in heaven." (3:22–4:1)

Before we look at Paul's instruction, it's a good idea to set out exactly what a bondservant was. The Greek word translated as "bondservant" can also be translated as "slave" or "servant." The translation of "bondservant" appears here in Colossians because it best fits the context of what Paul is teaching in this passage. A bondservant was someone bound under contract to serve a master for a set number of years, after which the person was declared free. Either way—bondservant or slave—those bound into these positions had few freedoms and were subject in every respect to the authority of their masters.

Paul guides those living in this social structure how to do so in a Christ-centered way. But we mustn't think that the stand Paul takes here implies approval of human bondage in any form. Reforming societal injustices wasn't his objective. Rather, his purpose was to set out how to live for Christ in any and every circumstance. In fact, Paul wrote an entire epistle, Philemon, to reconcile a slave and his master because they were brothers in Christ. The master, Philemon, was actually a member of the Colossian church. You might want to take a few minutes now to read that short epistle.

✦ How does Paul clarify, in 3:22–24, the way in which Christlike obedience springs from the heart, and how is this heart posture displayed in outward actions?

Paul gives a strong warning in 3:25 about what eventually happens to wrongdoers. He doesn't clarify whether the warning is directed to bondservants or masters, but it doesn't ultimately matter, because it applies to both. He is stating a general principle.

✦ In context, what does Paul's warning indicate about God's view of how we conduct ourselves in our various callings and responsibilities?

....

....

✢ Masters are to treat bondservants "justly and fairly" (4:1). What strong incentive does Paul provide for this fair treatment?

....

....

....

LET'S TALK

1. Lots of women bristle at Paul's instructions in 3:18: "Wives, submit to your husbands, as is fitting the Lord." Based on all Paul says—both in the household code of 3:18–4:1 and in his general instructions for Christian living in 3:1–17—discuss why his instructions to wives is "fitting." To help your discussion, you might also want to look at Ephesians 5:22–33 and 1 Peter 2:18–3:7.

....

....

....

....

....

....

....

2. Each one of us lives under the authority of others, whether at home or at work or at school. And as citizens, we are all under the authority of our governments. How does serving faithfully in a subordinate role demonstrate trust in God? Be sure to include in your discussion particular circumstances in which defying authority is actually the godly thing to do (see Acts 5:27–29).

WISE WALKING

COLOSSIANS 4:2-6

What do a woman in love, a business tycoon, and an Olympic athlete have in common? Obsession. Whether for love, wealth, or glory, the drive to experience or possess can, at times, become so preoccupying that everything else takes a back seat. For that reason, obsessions are rarely constructive in the long run. There's only one exception—an obsession with Christ, as Paul illustrates in his own life. His preoccupation with Christ compelled everything he did and how he did it. It dictated his prayers, his decisions, and all his relationships. It determined the details of his life and eventually his death. It caused him to flourish, not diminish. And it made him joyful rather than anxious. I want to be more like Paul, don't you? What a blessing, therefore, that as we study the Scriptures, including all we see and hear from Paul, the Holy Spirit is transforming us into Christ-obsessed women! But we have a part to play too, and we're given some very practical instructions this week, first about prayer and then about living in a way that makes the Christian life inviting to a skeptical world.

1. WATCHFUL PRAYER (4:2-4)

Prayer is Paul's first topic as he begins his final instructions:

> "Continue steadfastly in prayer, being watchful in it with thanksgiving. At the same time, pray also for us, that God may open to us a door for the word, to declare the mystery of Christ, on account of which I am in prison—that I may make it clear, which is how I ought to speak." (vv. 2–4)

✦ According to verse 2, what three qualities should characterize our prayer life?

1. ....

2. ....

3. ....

✦ What do we learn from the following passages about what it means to be watchful in prayer?

· Psalm 59:9

....

....

....

....

· Psalm 130:5–6

....

....

....

....

....

· Matthew 26:36–41

....

....

....

....

....

· 1 Peter 4:7

✦ After guiding the Colossians about how to pray, Paul adds his own prayer request. Considering his circumstances, which he mentions here in verse 3, what is notably absent from his request?

The word *mystery* appears here for the fourth time in the letter (we encountered it also in 1:26–27 and 2:2). The mystery once hidden but now revealed is that Christ and his gospel are being made known to all people, not just Jewish people. Paul's role in taking the gospel to these former outsiders is the reason he's in prison.

✦ How does Philippians 1:12–14 help us understand the heart of Paul's prayer request?

2. WISE WALKING (4:5)

The New Testament regularly applies the word *walk* to Christian living, just as Paul does here in verse 5:

"Walk in wisdom toward outsiders, making the best use of the time." (v. 5)

The term *walk* helps us picture the Christian life as a journey toward a set destination, our heavenly home. Here Paul has in mind a particular aspect of this journey, namely, taking part in making Christ known to those outside the faith.

✦ What aspect of wise walking does Paul identify in verse 5?

....

....

....

....

✦ Read Ephesians 5:15–21. How does this passage show us how to make the best use of time? List all the ways you see there.

....

....

....

....

✦ How do you think that our "walk," not just our words, serves to make Christ known?

....

....

....

....

3. SALTY SPEECH (4:6)

Our walk is to be a vital gospel witness, but our words—not just those about the gospel directly but all our words—must also reflect the grace and love of the Lord Jesus Christ:

> "Let your speech always be gracious, seasoned with salt, so that you may know how you ought to answer each person." (v. 6)

🕊 In Paul's day, salt was used as a food preservative as well as to add flavor, and he uses the word here with these functions in mind. His expression "seasoned with salt" modifies (is linked to) the preceding word he uses about speech. What particular "flavor" does Paul say is to characterize our speech?

....

....

....

....

🕊 How do the following passages enrich your understanding of Paul's instructions in verse 6?

· 1 Corinthians 10:31–33

....

....

....

....

· Ephesians 4:29

....

....

....

....

· 1 Peter 3:13–16

....

....

....

....

LET'S TALK

1. Have you ever been or are you currently obsessed with something or someone besides Christ? If so, how has the obsession impacted your responsibilities and relationships? Talk about why a Christ obsession produces very different fruit from other obsessions. Discuss what stands out to you about Paul's single-minded devotion, an aspect of it that you'd like for yourself. How can you cultivate it?

2. The way we live before unbelievers impacts how they view the gospel. Discuss Paul's blueprint for transparent living in verses 5–6. Include in your conversation specifically how you'll apply his instructions to walk in wisdom, to make the best use of your time, and to season your speech with salt.

LIVING IN CHRIST GROWS LOVE IN CHRIST

COLOSSIANS 4:7–18

As we come to the end of Colossians, we get a glimpse of the relational dynamics inside the church at Colossae and of the church's relationship with the apostle Paul. People are identified by name in these closing verses, some of whom we recognize from elsewhere in the New Testament and others who appear only here. But this is way more than a Bible history lesson. Paul's closing remarks and final greetings show us the trajectory of faithful ministry—where it leads and what it produces. Primarily, we're made to see the importance of Christians doing life in community, the God-given means through which we find encouragement, experience transformation, and develop enduring faith.

1. LIFE IN CHRIST ENCOURAGES (4:7–9)

Paul gets really personal here at the end of the letter, and in these closing remarks his overarching aim is to encourage the Colossian believers. He begins by naming the two men he is sending to Colossae on his behalf:

> Tychicus will tell you all about my activities. He is a beloved brother and faithful minister and fellow servant in the Lord. I have sent him to you for this very purpose, that you may know how we are and that he may encourage your hearts, and with him Onesimus, our faithful and beloved brother, who is one of you. They will tell you of everything that has taken place here. (vv. 7–9)

🌿 Tychicus was one of Paul's ministry partners (Acts 20:4) and the one Paul designated to carry this letter to Colossae. He also carried Paul's letters to the Ephesians and to Philemon. It's clear here that Tychicus was a gifted encourager. From verses 7 and 8, note the specific ways he provided encouragement:

· For Paul:

. . . .

. . . .

. . . .

. . . .

· For the Colossian believers:

. . . .

. . . .

. . . .

If you've read Paul's letter to Philemon, you recognize the name Onesimus. He was a bondservant or slave who had run away from his master Philemon. Then Onesimus was converted to Christ, and he somehow came into Paul's ministry. Afterward, Paul appealed to Philemon to welcome Onesimus back home and to receive him not as a wayward bondservant but as a brother in Christ. We are never told the outcome, but the fact that Paul sends Onesimus to the Colossian church, of which Philemon was a member, would seem to indicate that Philemon and Onesimus were reconciled, either before this occasion or sometime shortly afterward.

🌿 Read Philemon 8–12 and then compare what you see there with what Paul writes about Onesimus here in Colossians. How has faith in Christ and living among God's people changed Onesimus?

. . . .

. . . .

2. LIFE IN CHRIST TRANSFORMS (4:10-13)

Paul sends greetings from other ministry partners, three of whom were fellow Jews ("men of the circumcision") who had become Christ followers, and one of whom they knew already as an important figure in their very own church:

> "Aristarchus my fellow prisoner greets you, and Mark the cousin of Barnabas (concerning whom you have received instructions—if he comes to you, welcome him), and Jesus who is called Justus. These are the only men of the circumcision among my fellow workers for the kingdom of God, and they have been a comfort to me. Epaphras, who is one of you, a servant of Christ Jesus, greets you, always struggling on your behalf in his prayers, that you may stand mature and fully assured in all the will of God. For I bear him witness that he has worked hard for you and for those in Laodicea and in Hierapolis." (vv. 10–13)

The book of Acts tells us that Mark accompanied Paul on his first missionary journey, but at some point, Mark left the band of travelers. We aren't told why he left, but we do know that his leaving upset Paul, and it led to a falling out with Barnabas. Take a moment to read about that in Acts 15:36–41.

✠ With that relational backstory in mind, what seems to have changed based on what Paul writes here in verse 10?

✠ If you recall, Epaphras had been instrumental in grounding the Colossians in gospel truth and in establishing the Colossian church (take a look at Colossians 1:7–8 to refresh your memory). What does Paul tell us here about how Epaphras builds up the believers in Colossae and neighboring cities, and what is Epaphras's aim?

....

....

....

....

✤ What indication does Paul give in this passage as to how these ministry partners—the Jewish believers and Epaphras—have been and continue to be a source of strength for him as he sits in prison?

....

....

....

....

3. LIFE IN CHRIST PERSEVERES (4:14–18)

The remaining names on Paul's greetings list provide us with some insights into what enables Christians to persevere in their faith. We also find examples of what leads people to fall away. You are likely to recognize at least one name on the list:

> "Luke the beloved physician greets you, as does Demas. Give my greetings to the brothers at Laodicea, and to Nympha and the church in her house. And when this letter has been read among you, have it also read in the church of the Laodiceans; and see that you also read the letter from Laodicea. And say to Archippus, 'See that you fulfill the ministry that you have received in the Lord.' I, Paul, write this greeting with my own hand. Remember my chains. Grace be with you." (vv. 14–18)

Luke was a doctor by trade and the author of the Gospel that bears his name, as well as the book of Acts. Luke was not an eyewitness of Jesus's ministry, so his Gospel is based on secondhand information, but a good portion of the material in Acts comes firsthand since Luke was one of Paul's traveling companions.

✦ To get an idea of Luke's traveling experiences with Paul, read Acts 27:1–28:16. What do you notice in the story that no doubt helped the travelers to stick with their mission despite so many obstacles?

....

....

....

....

✦ Paul also sends greetings from Demas, one who, sadly, didn't persevere. According to 2 Timothy 4:10, what pulled him away from the Christian life and walking with God's people?

....

....

....

....

Nympha is another one Paul greets. Little is known about this woman beyond what we see here, that she hosted a church in her home. Mingled in this section are greetings to the Christians at Laodicea, along with Paul's request that his letters be shared between church locations.

✦ We hear more about the church at Laodicea at a later point, a time when the believers there weren't thriving as they seem to be at the time of this letter. Read Revelation 3:14–19.

· What led the believers in this church to compromise their Christian witness and walk of faith?

....

....

....

....

· What must they do in order to be restored to their earlier faithfulness?

....

....

....

....

· What encouragement is given in Revelation 3:19 to enable them to persevere?

....

....

....

....

✟ Before closing on a very personal note, Paul addresses Archippus, who might have been Philemon's son (see Philemon 2). We aren't told what prompted Paul's directive here, but whatever it was, Archippus clearly needed this word. Why do you think it is harder to persevere without such encouragement?

....

....

....

LET'S TALK

1. This week we considered the reconciliation of Onesimus and Philemon and that of Paul and Mark. What does this show us about how to please God in the way we handle our disagreements and relational fractures? Talk about the heart posture you need to repair such rifts. Pray that the Lord would open your heart to see any relational breaks in your own life and give you both humility and wisdom for how to proceed.

2. It's clear from the way that Paul refers to Luke in Colossians 4:14 that he valued their partnership. They'd shared a lot of hardship and together had seen the Lord's faithfulness again and again. Discuss how friendship bonds form around shared faith and ministry. Where have you experienced this?

3. As we come to the end of Colossians, note what you've learned or what's affected you most about:

· the character of God

· the gospel of salvation through Jesus Christ

· the path of discipleship

HELPFUL RESOURCES FOR
STUDYING COLOSSIANS

Beale, G. K. *Colossians and Philemon*. Baker Exegetical Commentary on the New Testament. Grand Rapids, MI: Baker, 2019.

Hughes, R. Kent. *Philippians, Colossians, and Philemon: The Fellowship of the Gospel and the Supremacy of Christ*. Preaching the Word. Edited by R. Kent Hughes. Wheaton, IL: Crossway, 2013.

Johnston, Mark G. *Let's Study Colossians and Philemon*. Let's Study Series. Edinburgh: Banner of Truth, 2013.

McFadden, Kevin W. *Hidden with Christ in God: A Theology of Colossians and Philemon*. New Testament Theology. Edited by Thomas R. Schreiner and Brian S. Rosner. Wheaton, IL: Crossway, 2023.

Wilson, Alistair I. "Colossians." In *Ephesians–Philemon*, edited by Iain M. Duguid, James M. Hamilton Jr., and Jay Sklar, 197–255. Vol. 11 of ESV Expository Commentary. Wheaton, IL: Crossway, 2018.

NOTES

1. "The Setting of Colossians" map from page 2292 of the ESV® Study Bible (The Holy Bible, English Standard Version®), copyright © 2008 by Crossway, a publishing ministry of Good News Publishers. Used by permission. All rights reserved.

2. *Merriam-Webster*, s.v. "metaphor," accessed April 6, 2023, http://www.merriam-webster.com/dictionary/metaphor.

3. ESV® Study Bible, note on Rev. 3:14.

4. J. I. Packer, cited in Alistair I. Wilson, "Colossians," in *Ephesians–Philemon*, ESV Expository Commentary, vol. 11, ed. Iain M. Duguid, James M. Hamilton Jr., and Jay Sklar (Wheaton, IL: Crossway, 2018), 227.

5. ESV® Study Bible (Wheaton, IL: Crossway, 2008), note on Col. 1:25.

6. "The Riches of God's Mystery," Ligonier Ministries, January 28, 2011, https://www.ligonier.org/.

7. Ligon Duncan, "The Incomparable Christ: Exposition of Colossians VIII," sermon, Reformed Theological Seminary website, October 20, 1996, https://rts.edu/resources/.

8. ESV® Study Bible, note on 1 Pet. 4:1–2.

9. Barry Cooper, "Incarnation," Ligonier Ministries, April 13, 2021, https://www.ligonier.org/podcasts/simply-put/incarnation.

10. ESV® Study Bible, note on Col. 2:14.

11. ESV® Study Bible, note on Col. 2:12–13.

12. Wilson, "Colossians," 238.

13. *Merriam-Webster*, s.v. "asceticism," accessed April 18, 2023, http://www.merriam-webster.com/dictionary/asceticism.

14. John Piper, "Flesh Tank and Peashooter Regulations," sermon, January 17, 1982, Desiring God, https://www.desiringgod.org/.

15. "The Loss and Restoration of Liberty," Ligonier Ministries, April 24, 2017, https://www.ligonier.org/.

16. ESV® Study Bible, note on Eph. 6:2–3.

Flourish Bible Study Series